Grammar Success

3

SoPHia Rafiq

Raising Writing Standards

Pie Corbett   Rachel Roberts

OXFORD

OXFORD
UNIVERSITY PRESS

Great Clarendon Street, Oxford OX2 6DP

Oxford University Press is a department of the University of Oxford.
It furthers the University's objective of excellence in research, scholarship,
and education by publishing worldwide in

Oxford New York

Auckland Bangkok Buenos Aires Cape Town Chennai
Dar es Salaam Delhi Hong Kong Istanbul Karachi Kolkata
Kuala Lumpur Madrid Melbourne Mexico City Mumbai Nairobi
São Paulo Shanghai Singapore Taipei Tokyo Toronto

and associated company in Berlin

Oxford is a registered trade mark of Oxford University Press
in the UK and in certain other countries

British Library Cataloguing in Publication Data

Data available

ISBN 0 19 834287 X

10 9 8 7 6 5 4 3 2 1

Typeset and designed by Oxford Designers & Illustrators

Printed in Hong Kong

With thanks to Nicky Theobold, Mary Duke and the 'Foxes' of Marshfield
Primary School for the children's work featured on the cover of *Grammar
Success 3*.

Preface

Grammar Success is about teaching children how to use grammar to improve their writing. It provides materials, not only to deepen children's grammatical understanding, but also to refine their grammatical skills and to enable them to apply these to their own writing.

The course is built around the National Literacy Framework sentence level objectives. However, where there are gaps in the framework (for instance, the omission of nouns from Year 3) these have been addressed. Each unit is broken down into three sessions, based around the pupils' book, *Teacher's Guide* and the *Overhead Transparency Pack*.

Session 1 uses an OHT to introduce the grammatical objective to the children. This part of the session should be lively, and interactive. Children then deepen their understanding of the particular grammatical feature through various independent activities. By the end of Session 1, pupils should be in a position to define their understanding of the objective.

Session 2 uses the pupils' book unit, plus photocopiable activities in the *Teacher's Guide*. Pupils focus upon the grammatical feature in the context of wide-ranging stimulus texts. The children are asked comprehension questions on each text before moving into activities that focus upon the grammatical feature in use. By the end of this session, pupils have critically reflected upon the use of the objective through their reading.

Session 3 relates again to the text in the pupils' book, which now becomes a model for children's own writing. The teacher's notes describe in detail how to carry out shared writing, demonstrating how to use the grammatical feature in the process of writing a new text. A photocopiable Reminder Sheet in the *Teacher's Guide* provides a summary, defining the grammatical feature and giving guidance on how to use it effectively in writing. It can be used for activities flagged by the symbol |Ꭱ|. The session ends with pupils producing their own work, drawing on the shared writing experience.

Session 4 provides an opportunity to develop writing skills, embedding the grammatical feature into the child's repertoire as a writer. This may involve revisiting and refining what was written in the third session, building upon notes or a plan already begun, or by writing a further example in the light of what was written in session 3. It is important to revisit and refine children's usage of any grammatical point so that it becomes part and parcel of their ongoing writing.

While a full range of texts and outcomes are provided in the pupils' book, children will gain greater understanding of the grammar if all three elements of the course are available to them.

Activities are differentiated in both the pupils' book (A–C) and *Teacher's Guide* to allow for pupils who may struggle or who need an extra challenge. The photocopiable activities double as a valuable homework resource.

The course helps pupils to understand grammar but also to become skilful in the key grammatical skills of:

- sentence construction
- punctuation
- enhancing writing with different language effects
- cohesion – links with and between sentences, paragraphs and texts.

The more adept children are at using these skills in their writing, the more freedom they will have to focus upon the act of creative composition.

Pie Corbett

Sources

The texts used in this book are extracted from the following full sources, and we are grateful for their permission to reproduce copyright material.

p 10   Extract from *Stig of the Dump* by Clive King (Puffin, 1963), copyright © Clive King 1963, reprinted by permission of Penguin Books Ltd.

p 12   Extract from *Crummy Mummy and Me* by Anne Fine, and front cover illustration by David Higham (Puffin, 1989), text copyright © Anne Fine 1988 illustration copyright © David Higham 1988, reprinted by permission of Penguin Books Ltd.

p 18   Extract from *To Kill a Mocking Bird* by Harper Lee (Heinemann, 1960), reprinted by permission of The Random House Group Ltd; and extract from *The Giant Goldfish Robbery* by Richard Kidd (Corgi Yearling, 1999), copyright © Richard Kidd 1999, reprinted by permission of David Higham Associates Ltd.

p 20   Extract from *A Long Way from Chicago* by Richard Peck (Hodder Children's Books, 2000), reprinted by permission of the publisher, Hodder and Stoughton Ltd.

p 22   Extract from *Toad Rage* by Morris Gleitzman (Penguin Books, Australia, 1999), reprinted by permission of the publisher.

p 24   Extract from *The Return of the Naked Chef* by Jamie Oliver (Michael Joseph, 2000), copyright © Jamie Oliver Ltd, 2000, reprinted by permission of Penguin Books Ltd. Photography by David Loftus copyright © David Loftus 2000, reprinted by permission of the photographer.

p 26   Extract from *Beowolf and the Monster* by Brian Patten (Scholastic Children's Books, 1999), reprinted by permission of the publisher.

p 28   Lines from 'Colonel Fazackerly' by Charles Causley from *Going to the Fair* (Viking, 1994), reprinted by permission of David Higham Associates Ltd.

p 30   'The Raven and the Whale' from *The Song of Birds* collected and retold by Hugh Lupton (Barefoot Books, 2000), reprinted by permission of the publisher.

p 34   Extract from 'The Heartless Giant' by Jim Henson from *The Storyteller* (Boxtree, an imprint of Macmillan Publishers Ltd, 1992), reprinted by permission of the publishers.

p 36   'Fish in the Forest' from *Tales of Wisdom and Wonder* retold by Hugh Lupton (Barefoot Books, 1998), reprinted by permission of the publisher.

p 38   Extract from *The Oxford Children's Pocket Encyclopedia* (OUP, 2000), reprinted by permission of Oxford University Press.

p 40   Extract from *Creative Storytelling* by Jack Zipes (Routledge, 1995), reprinted by permission of Routledge, Inc., part of The Taylor & Francis Group and illustration from *The Pied Piper of Hamelin* by Val Biro (Oxford University Press, 1985), copyright © Val Biro 1985, reprinted by permission of the author/illustrator.

p 44   Extract from report by Mark Tully from *Second Sight* campaign leaflet, copyright © Mark Tully 1999, first published in *The Guardian*, Spring 1999, reprinted by permission of the author; illustrations by Chris Molan, copyright © OUP 2000, from *Creatures, Kings and Scary Things* (OUP 2000), reprinted by permission of Oxford University Press

p 46   Extract from *The Jungle Book* by Rudyard Kipling (Macmillan Centenary Edition, 1982), reprinted by permission of A P Watt Ltd on behalf of The National Trust for Places of Historical Interest or Natural Beauty.

p 48   Extract from http://www.vegsoc.org/health (The Vegetarian Society), reprinted with their permission.

p 50   'Billy McBone' by Allan Ahlberg from *Heard it in the Playground* (Viking, 1989), copyright © Allan Ahlberg 1989, reprinted by permission of Penguin Books Ltd.

p 52   Extract from *The Voyage of the Dawn Treader* by C.S. Lewis (Clive Staples, 1952), copyright © C.S. Lewis Pte Ltd 1952, reprinted by permission of The C.S. Lewis Company Ltd.

p 56   Extract from *Harry Potter and the Philosopher's Stone* by J K Rowling (Bloomsbury, 1997), copyright © J.K. Rowling 1997, reprinted by permission of Christopher Little Literary Agency.

Contents

TERM 3

UNIT

Story openings

Under the cold dark waters of the loch, two hundred metres down, mattressed on mud and blanketed with slime, a boggart lay sleeping.

(From *The Boggart and the Monster* by Susan Cooper)

Sometimes at night when the rain is beating against the windows of my room, I think about that summer on the farm.

(From *The Midnight Fox* by Betsy Byars)

There was a dragon in the sky the night before the stranger came.

(From *The Fated Sky* by Henrietta Branford)

'Too many!' James shouted, and slammed the door behind him.

(From *The Dark is Rising* by Susan Cooper)

IN THE OLD DAYS, when this story took place, time used to run by clockwork.

(From *Clockwork* by Philip Pullman)

'Uncle Bart,' said Limpy. 'Why do humans hate us?'

(From *Toad Rage* by Morris Gleitzman)

'Our last moments of freedom,' Lloyd said darkly.

(From *The Demon Headmaster* by Gillian Cross)

Two men sat on a bench on the ice.

The middle of the night, and everyone in the house asleep. Everyone? Then what was that noise?

(From *The Battle of Bubble and Squeak* by Philippa Pearce)

(From *Flain's Coronet* by Catherine Fisher)

These are opening lines from different stories. Read them through and discuss the following questions.

1 Which of the openings do you think is the most successful and why?

2 Thinking about the text you have chosen in question 1, how does the writer use the opening lines:
- to create an atmosphere?
- to set the scene?
- to introduce a character?
- to be dramatic?
- to intrigue the reader?
- to create a strong picture in the reader's mind?

3 Categorize the openings and imitate them. For instance, this is an exclamation opening – *'Too many!' James shouted, and slammed the door behind him.* It could be imitated in this way – *'No way!' Sam yelled, and ran down the garden.*

4 Rewrite each story opening by moving the words, phrases or clauses around. For instance, *There was a dragon in the sky the night before the stranger came* could become, *In the night sky, before the stranger came, there was a dragon* or *The night before the stranger came, there was a dragon in the sky* or *Before the stranger came, there was a dragon in the night sky.* You may need to make slight alterations to some words.

5 In pairs, discuss the effect of altering the word order and decide which sentence construction is the most powerful.

6 Write the beginning paragraphs for a story, using one of the opening categories that you have been working on. Remember to think about the impact and flow of your writing and check that it makes good sense.

Using standard English

Stig of the Dump

He came out of the shack and faced the Snargets. One had a broken-down old airgun, and the others were pointing sticks.

'Cor! It ain't Albert!' exclaimed the youngest Snarget.

'We can see that!' said the oldest roughly.

'What's yer name?' he said to Barney in the same voice.

'Barney,' said Barney. 'What's yours?'

'I'm the Lone Ranger and 'e's Robin Hood and 'e's William Tell,' snapped the eldest Snarget.

'Golly,' exclaimed Barney.

'Quiet!' snapped the first Snarget. 'What was you doin' in our shack?'

'Yes, and watcher mean by chuckin' dirt at us?' asked the second Snarget.

'Yes, and watcher doin' in our dump anyway?' piped the youngest fiercely.

'Can if I want to,' replied Barney, pretending not to mind. But he was not really feeling very comfortable. He was not sure just how rough these Snargets could get.

'"Can if 'e wants to!", 'e says!' exclaimed the Lone Ranger as if he couldn't believe his ears. 'What shall we do wiv 'im, fellers?'

'Tie 'im to a tree and shoot 'im full of arrers,' suggested Robin Hood.

'Put 'im in a dungeon and leave 'im to rot,' said William Tell.

'No, I reckon we ought to lynch 'im on the spot. String 'im up!' said the Lone Ranger masterfully.

'We ain't got no rope,' said Robin Hood.

'Well, we ain't got no bowsanarrers,' pointed out William Tell.

'Well, there certainly ain't no dungeons for miles around,' said the Lone Ranger. 'Let's just give 'im a bit of Slow Torture.'

'You wouldn't dare!' said Barney. But he didn't feel too sure.

'Oh, wouldn't we!' sneered the Lone Ranger. 'That's what you think. We often do, don't we fellers? Do it all the time, don't we, give people the Slow Torture?'

'Yes. And shoot 'em full of arrers,' agreed Robin Hood.

'Yes. And put 'em in dungeons,' added William Tell.

'I'd tell a policeman,' said Barney stoutly.

The eldest Snarget looked carefully around the pit. 'Can't see no policeman 'ere,' he said scornfully.

'I'd tell my Granny, and she lives just up there,' said Barney. The Snargets collapsed in howls of laughter.

'"'E'd tell 'is Granny," 'e says! 'Ear that fellers! 'E'd tell 'is Granny!' they cackled.

Barney felt his face going red and tears coming into his eyes. Then he thought of something. 'I'm going to tell Stig,' he said calmly.

(From *Stig of the Dump* by Clive King)

Read the passage through and answer the following questions.

1 Why do the Snargets say that they are the Lone Ranger, Robin Hood and William Tell? Give two reasons.

2 In which three ways does Barney try to talk his way out of trouble?

3 What does the word *stoutly* suggest that Barney might be feeling and thinking?

4 Why do you think the Snargets cackle about Barney telling his Granny?

5 Find five places where the altered spelling shows the Snargets' pronunciation, e.g. *yer* is you, *'e* is he.

6 Rewrite the text, from *Yes, and watcher doin' in our dump* to *We ain't got no rope*. This is where the writer has used spelling to show the accents of the Snargets. Rewrite using the correct spelling to change how the Snargets speak. Read it aloud to hear the difference and discuss how this changes the Snargets. For instance, '"'E'd tell 'is Granny," 'e says!' becomes '"*He would tell his Grandmother*," *he says!*'

7 Find two places where the Snargets use non-standard English. Remember – do not muddle this with where the writer has changed the spelling of a word to show how it is spoken. You are looking for places where the grammar of the sentence is non-standard. For instance, if you think of the sentence *I like them books,* the word *them* is non-standard English and should say *those.*

|R|

8 Continue the conversation between Barney and the Snargets. Before doing this, make a list of possible non-standard English expressions that they might use. Work in pairs to prepare a dialogue between Barney and the chief Snarget. Aim for a contrast between the two characters by using different accents, and by using standard and non-standard English.

Improving your writing

Crummy Mummy and Me

At last, she comes downstairs. And even then she's never dressed right. You'd think, honestly you would, that we didn't have any windows upstairs, the way she chooses what to wear. She certainly can't bother to look through them at the weather. She'll sail down in midwinter, when it's snowing, in a thin cotton frock with short puffy sleeves, and no woolly.

I have to be firm.

"You can't come out like that."

"Why not?"

"You just can't," I tell her. "You'll catch your death. It's snowing out there. It's *far* too cold for bare arms. You'll freeze."

"I'll put a coat on."

But I just stare at her until she goes back upstairs for a sweater. And even then she'll choose something quite unsuitable. She never dresses in the right sort of thing. She'd wear her glittery legwarmers to a funeral if I let her (or if we ever went to funerals). She'd sit on a beach in her thick purple poncho. If she were called in to see the headmaster, she'd rather wear those baggy flowery shorts she found abandoned on a park bench last Easter than anything sensible. She'd look fantastic – she always does – but not at all like a mother. You have to watch her. You can't let up.

At least she admits it.

"I'm a terrible embarrassment to you, Mina," she confesses, buckling on two of her best studded belts. "I'm a Crummy Mummy."

Then I feel mean for being so stern.

(From *Crummy Mummy and Me* by Anne Fine)

This passage comes from the first chapter of *Crummy Mummy and Me* by Anne Fine. Read it through and answer the following.

1 List three reasons why Mina might be critical of the way in which Crummy Mummy dresses.

2 Why do you think Mina feels mean for being so stern?

3 Why do you think Mina's mum describes herself as a Crummy Mummy?

4 Which is the main clause in each of the following sentences?
   (a) *I just stare at her until she goes back upstairs for a sweater.*
   (b) *If she were called in to see the headmaster, she'd rather wear those baggy flowery shorts than anything sensible.*

   Rewrite sentence (b) in several different ways, creating more than one sentence if you wish. Which of your versions is easier to read and why?

5 Take a paragraph from a previous story that you have written. Reread it and think about how effective the writing sounds. What improvements and corrections could you make to the story to make it more readable?

6 Rewrite the first paragraph of *Crummy Mummy and Me* to alter the impact of the writing. You might wish to:
   (a) add words in to enrich description,
   (b) extend sentences, for instance by using connectives,
   (c) change words for effect,
   (d) rewrite or trim particular constructions.

7 Write another incident in which the roles of parent and child are reversed. This could be a meal time, or Mina wanting to go up to bed and Crummy Mummy wanting her to stay up late and play! As you write, reread and consider ways to improve your writing.

Adapting a playscript

A CUT TOO FAR!

Daisy (*holding up a Barbie doll that has been shaved bald*)
Right, which of you is responsible?

Poppy (*shrugging her shoulders*) Not me.

Tony Me neither.

Daisy Well, one of you must have done it 'cos I don't see Mum
or Dad shaving the hair off my Barbie.

Tony Well it wasn't us. So take your scraggy doll and clear off.

Daisy Oh thanks, I see that Mr Sympathetic is at home today.

Poppy Maybe your so-called friend Hayley did it when you
were out of the room. After all, you have had an
argument with her.

Daisy Hayley would never dare.

Poppy If you're that bothered you can have one of my old
Barbies. I don't play with them anymore.

Daisy I don't want an old one – I want my new one back.
Complete with hair.

Tony Stop fussing about and just glue the hair back on.

Daisy I can't glue it back on. It won't be the same. It's ruined.
One of you must know something.

(*no-one answers*)

Daisy OK. I'll go and find Mum. (*calling off stage*) Mum, Mum!

Mum What is that dreadful shouting for?

Daisy Somebody's ruined my Barbie.

Mum (*crossly*) Right you two.
Who did this?

Pie Corbett

Read the passage through and answer the following questions.

1 What do you think has just happened in the play before this extract?

2 Why do you think this?

3 Who is more sympathetic – Tony or Poppy?

4 What clue makes you think this?

5 Work in fours to prepare a reading of the extract.

Remember to pay attention to the stage directions.

6 Rewrite the first four lines as if this were part of a diary written in the first person, from Daisy's point of view. You could begin, *I stormed into the room, holding up a Barbie doll…*

7 Rewrite Poppy's reply that begins, *Maybe your so-called friend…* as if it were from Poppy's diary. You could begin, *'So, I turned to Daisy and…'*

8 Invent a newspaper headline for this event.

9 Work in fours to create the next scene in which the culprit admits to shaving the doll.

10 Rewrite the incidents in the play as a story written in the third person. Try to show how the characters think and feel – the stage directions will help you with this. After you have written your story extract, make a list of three ways you had to adapt the words and sentences from the original playscript. Continue writing the story using the scene you prepared for question 9, in which the culprit owns up. Remember, the story should tell what happened *and* how the characters think and feel.

Direct & reported speech

ANOTHER FOOD UPSET

Sarah Dunk was charged with having committed the following assault on Saturday morning last on the matron of the Battle workhouse.

The matron examined: On Saturday morning as we were about assembling for the purpose of attending Divine service I went into the kitchen as is my usual custom and there I saw Sarah Dunk with a can full of gruel and some bread in her hands; she was eating it. It was after she had had her breakfast; it was a quart can of gruel, and more than the usual allowance. I have frequently observed Sarah Dunk have more food than the rest of the inmates; I judge this must have been given her by some of the rest. On this occasion, I said 'Sarah, give me that gruel.' She replied that she would not. I then attempted to take it from her, when a scuffle ensued, my thumb got entangled in the handle of the can. And it was much bruised and caused me for some time considerable pain. She declared I should not have the gruel; she would throw it upon the floor first, and at last the can was upset and fell upon the floor. The scuffle continued from the kitchen into the wash-house where I was struck repeatedly. She tore my cap and her own too. (Witness produced the caps.) Her general conduct is exceedingly bad. I fear she is urged to conduct herself in this manner by others.

Dunk, in her defence, stated that her mistress struck her first and had struck her twice before.

This was proved to be untrue, and the magistrates sentenced the prisoner to 14 days' imprisonment in Battle gaol, and recommended her to the especial care of Cook, the keeper, who intimated that there would be no dispute about the 'gruel' in his quarters.

The Brighton Guardian 22 February 1837

This is from an English newspaper written in 1837. It describes an event in a workhouse. Workhouses were places where very poor people were kept. Read the passage through and answer the following.

1 Who gave the most evidence? Suggest two reasons why this might have been so.

2 Give two reasons why Sarah Dunk might have been given food by other inmates.

3 Why does the matron think that Sarah behaves badly?

4 How do you think the magistrates managed to 'prove' that Sarah was lying, given the evidence reported.

5 What impression do get of the keeper, 'Cook'?

6 Find one place where matron reports what Sarah said. Rewrite this as direct speech, giving the actual words that you think Sarah might have spoken.

7 Rewrite the first paragraph as if it were from a story. Use direct speech. Begin with the following words, *The matron stood up ready to begin. 'Repeat these words after me,' said the foreman holding out the Bible…*

8 Using direct speech and basing your ideas on the final paragraph, rewrite what the keeper, Cook, might have said in court. Start with the words, *Cook, the keeper, stood up, and stared at the magistrate. He spoke in a loud clear voice, with his hands gripping the edge of the bench, his knuckles whitening…*

9 Rewrite what you think Sarah Dunk might have said in her defence. Write this in direct speech but use some reported speech to indicate what was said by the matron and Sarah during the incident. Use what the matron said of the incident but make sure that you alter events to make Sarah seem a better character. Begin with Sarah explaining to the magistrates why she needed extra food.

Using punctuation

Setting the scene

MAYCOMB was an old town, but it was a tired old town when I first knew it. In rainy weather the streets turned to red slop; grass grew on the sidewalks; the court-house sagged in the square. Somehow, it was hotter then; a black dog suffered on a summer's day; bony mules hitched to Hoover carts flicked flies in the sweltering shade of the live oaks on the square. Men's stiff collars wilted by nine in the morning. Ladies bathed before noon, after their three o'clock naps, and by nightfall were like soft tea-cakes with frostings of sweat and sweet talcum.

(From *To Kill a Mocking-Bird* by Harper Lee)

When I close my eyes I can still hear the mad squawking of the seagulls, the slushing noises of the crushed ice and the whirring of the fork-lift trucks. I can see the rainbow shimmering of the herrings, the gold and black, glassy eyes of the freckled cod and the ghostly white underbellies of the giant skate.

(From *The Giant Goldfish Robbery* by Richard Kidd)

These are passages from the opening chapters of different stories. Read them through and answer the following questions.

1 In the first passage, how did the rain affect Maycomb?

2 How did men and women suffer in the hot weather?

3 Give two clues that suggest that the second passage is set on the coast.

4 From the second passage, list one memory that the main character can still see and one that he can hear.

5 In the second passage the author creates two lists, using commas. In one he lists what the main character could remember hearing and in the other what he could see. Notice how he uses detail. Use the same sentence structure to write two sentences about where you live.
e.g. *When I close my eyes I can still hear the overhead rumble of planes, the sparrows arguing in the trees and the angry lawn mowers on Sunday afternoons. I can see the purple Buddleia, the sharp, spiked thistle and the late-night cars like a necklace of light down our road.*

6 In the first passage Harper Lee uses a semi-colon to link sentences together and build up the description of the town, in a dramatic way. Thinking about where you live, imitate the first passage using the same sentence structure as the first line. Then, using semi-colons, add description as in the second and third sentences. Follow this by showing how different people react to the town, selecting words carefully and using similes where possible.
e.g. *Stroud is an old town, but it was a weary old town when I knew it, like an old relative. When the sun shone the streets blistered; dogs slept in the graveyard, resting in cool shadows; the elderly toiled up the High Street, pausing for breath. When it snowed the wind cut into you; toddlers ran red-faced, skating on the pavements; cars skidded homewards. Teenagers stood on street corners eyeing the world as if it was about to pounce on them.*

Writing dialogue

A long way from Chicago

He was a big, tall galoot of a kid with narrow eyes. His gaze kept flitting to the shotgun. The uniform he had on was all white with a cap to match. In his hand was a wire holder for milk bottles. He was ready to make his escape, but Grandma was saying, 'I hope I have better luck with your milk today than the last batch. I found a dead mouse in your delivery yesterday.'

The kid's eyes widened. 'Naw you never,' he said.

'Be real careful about calling a customer a liar,' she remarked. 'I had to feed milk to the cat. And the mouse too, of course.'

'Naw,' the kid said, reaching around for the knob on the screen door behind him.

Grandma was telling one of her whoppers. If she'd found a mouse in the milk, she'd have exploded like the mailbox. She was telling a whopper, and I wondered why.

'And another thing,' she said. 'I won't be needing a delivery tomorrow, neither milk nor cream. I'm going away.'

First we'd heard of it. Mary Alice nudged me hard.

'I'll be gone tonight and all day tomorrow, and I don't want milk left out where it'll sour. I won't pay for it. I'm taking my grandkids on a visit to my cousin Leota Shrewsbury.'

Another whopper, and a huge one. Grandma off on a jaunt and us with her? I didn't think so. She didn't do things that cost. And she never told anybody her business.

Turning from the stove, she pretended surprise at seeing Mary Alice and me there, though she had eyes in the back of her head. 'Why, there's my grandkids now.' She pointed us out with a spatula. 'They're from Chicago. Gangs run that town, you know,' she told the kid. 'My grandson's in a gang, so you don't want to mess with him. He's meaner than he looks.'

I hung in the doorway, bug-eyed and short. She was saying I – Joey Dowdel – was a tough guy from Chicago, and this kid was twice my size. He could eat me for lunch.

'This here's Ernie Cowgill,' she said, finishing off the introductions. With a sneer at me, Ernie Cowgill disappeared through the door and stomped off the porch.

'Grandma,' I croaked, 'you'll get me killed.'

(From *A Long Way From Chicago* by Richard Peck)

Read the passage through and answer the following.

1 What do you think 'galoot' means?

2 Write four things that you know about Ernie, quoting from the text.

3 Give two reasons why Ernie is keen to get out of the house.

4 Write three things that you know about Grandma, quoting from the text. Why does Grandma tell lies to Ernie?

5 How does the author suggest, towards the end, that Ernie might not have believed Grandma's story?

6 Find two examples where the writer gives a supporting action before or after what is spoken.
   e.g. *'Why, there's my grandkids now.' She pointed us out with a spatula.*

7 Copy the sentence pattern, inventing a different situation.
   e.g. *'Why, there's my dog now.' She grabbed Rover by the collar.*

8 Find an example where a character speaks and the writer follows this by giving another character's reactions or thoughts.
   e.g. *'This here's Ernie Cowgill,' she said, finishing off the introductions. With a sneer at me, Ernie Cowgill disappeared through the door and stomped off the porch.*

9 Copy the sentence pattern, inventing a different situation.
   e.g. *'This is Sam Dawes,' she muttered, staring out of the window. With a sniff in my direction, Miss Dawes gathered her skirts and flounced out.*

R

10 Write a further episode in which Ernie delivers milk to Grandma, and she boasts about Mary Alice. Remember to keep the characters in role. When writing dialogue think carefully about vocabulary. Try to include supporting actions, or a character's reaction to what is said.

Verbs for character & action

TOAD RAGE

'Uncle Bart,' said Limpy. 'Why do humans hate us?'

Uncle Bart looked down at Limpy and smiled fondly.

'Stack me, Limpy,' he chuckled, 'you are an idiot.'

Limpy felt his warts prickle with indignation as Uncle Bart hopped onto the road after a bull ant.

No wonder I've never heard any other cane toad ask that question, thought Limpy, if that's the reply you get.

Limpy was glad the grass at the edge of the highway was taller than he was. At least the millions of insects flying around the railway crossing light couldn't see who Uncle Bart was calling an idiot.

'Humans don't hate us,' Uncle Bart was saying, his mouth full of bull ant and grasshopper. 'What are you on about? Stack me, some of the dopey ideas you youngsters come up with…'

Limpy waited patiently for Uncle Bart to finish. Uncle Bart was his fattest uncle, and his bossiest. When Uncle Bart had a point to make, he liked to keep on making it until you gave in and looked convinced.

Tonight, though, Limpy didn't give in.

He didn't have to. While Uncle Bart was getting his mucus in a knot about how humans definitely didn't hate cane toads, a truck came roaring round the corner in a blaze of lights, straightened up, rumbled across the road straight at Uncle Bart and drove over him.

Limpy trembled in the grass while the truck thundered past in a cloud of diesel fumes and flying grit. Then he hopped onto the road and looked down at what was left of Uncle Bart.

The light overhead was very bright because it had a whole railway crossing to illuminate, and Limpy was able to see very clearly that Uncle Bart wasn't his fattest uncle any more.

Flattest more like, he thought sadly.

'See,' he said quietly to Uncle Bart. 'That's what I'm on about.'

'Har har har,' chortled a nearby grasshopper. 'Your uncle's a placemat. Serves him right.'

(From *Toad Rage* by Morris Gleitzman)

These are opening lines from Morris Gleitzman's book *Toad Rage*. Read them through and answer the following.

1 List ways in which the writer makes an impact on the reader in this opening.

2 How does Limpy feel when Uncle Bart calls him an idiot?

3 Find ways in which the writer shows us that Uncle Bart is bossy.

4 Why is Limpy glad the grass is tall?

5 How do you know that Uncle Bart was wrong to believe that humans *don't hate us*.

6 Find a speech verb to show how Uncle Bart feels.

7 List the verbs that show how the truck behaved.

8 Find the verb that shows how Limpy reacted to Uncle Bart's death.

9 Which verb suggests that the grasshopper did not care about Uncle Bart's demise?

10 Rewrite the paragraph that begins *He didn't have to* in the present tense. Compare this with the original, which is written in the past tense. Which do you think sounds more effective and why?

11 Continue the dialogue between Limpy and the grasshopper. Show how sad Limpy is feeling. Contrast this with the chirpy, and rather cheeky, grasshopper. Limpy is concerned to discover why humans do not like cane toads and to find ways of helping the toads cross the road safely. Select verbs carefully in the dialogue to show the different characters and what they do. A useful fact that may help you round off the chapter is that cane toads eat grasshoppers!

Writing instructions

Imperatives – the bossy verbs

pan-toasted almonds with a touch of chilli and sea salt

These must be the quickest thing in the world to make. Believe me, there's nothing more scrumptious with any cold drink and good company than a plate of hot, toasted, tasty almonds. Try throwing them into salads too – nothing better.

serves 8
½ tablespoon olive oil
255g/9oz shelled and peeled almonds
1–3 small dried red chillies
2 generous pinches of Maldon sea salt

Add the olive oil and almonds to a hot frying pan. Fry and kinda toast the almonds until golden brown, shaking the pan regularly to colour them evenly and accentuate their nutty flavour. Crumble in the chilli to taste and add the sea salt. Toss over and serve hot on a large plate. Bloomin' gorgeous.

(From *The Return of the Naked Chef* by Jamie Oliver)

Read this set of instructions and answer the following questions.

1   Do you think you would like to try this dish or not? Why?

2   Why do you think the recipe title does not use capital letters?

3   How does the writing change between the three sections?

4   Find two examples of where the writer is making the instructions sound informal, and breaks the normal conventions of recipe writing.

5   Who do you think Jamie Oliver is writing for and why do you think this?

6   What tense is this recipe written in?

7   If this were to be rewritten as a recount about how you cooked this dish, what tense would you use – and why?

8   Find four sentences that begin with imperative verbs, instructing the reader in what to do.

9   Rewrite the first paragraph, making it sound more like a conventional introduction to a recipe.

10 Rewrite the third paragraph making it easier for the reader to follow the instructions. You could use bullet points, numbers or letters, and illustrations, as well as changing the sentences, for instance by adding connectives such as 'first'. You might wish to split some of the sentences to make the sequence easier to read.

11 Write a recipe for your favourite snack. Imitate the way in which Jamie Oliver writes, mixing a friendly, informal style to appeal to the reader. At the same time, make sure that the ingredients needed are clearly presented and that the instructions are well set out. Use imperative verbs to instruct the reader.

Creating different emphases

Beowulf and the Monster

Centuries ago, when the land was covered in forests and wolves and demons crouched in every shadow, there lived a powerful warrior king. He was as famous for his generosity as for his strength, and when his last great battle was over and peace declared, he decided to hold a wonderful party to celebrate.

He sent out invitations to the rich and poor alike, and then set about building a gigantic hall in which to hold his special feast. All his people came to help him build the hall, from the oldest to the youngest, and the new building rose quickly in a vast clearing in the forest.

It was a majestic hall, with wooden towers and pinnacles that reached higher than the highest trees. It was the tallest, finest building that had ever been seen in the land. And the king was proud of it. Nothing as grand had existed in his kingdom before. It became known as the Great Hall.

As soon as the Hall was finished the party began. It was to be the feast to end all feasts. It began one morning as the sun rose and then continued day after day, night after night. Long tables sagged under the weight of the food, and the revellers sagged under the effect of the drink. It made their heads spin and caused them to sing louder and to dance more wildly.

All this happened in the distant times, when wild boars roamed the countryside, and moon-mad wolves slunk through the night. It was a time when the world was heaped with mysteries.

The feast was a roaring success. The music and singing grew louder and louder, and the louder it became the farther the sound travelled, until it was heard beyond the forest by the one being whom no one in their wildest dreams would have invited to the feast.

It was heard by the monster, Grendel.

Grendel lived in the fens and the foul-smelling marshland beyond the forest. The marsh was littered with oozing pools and the festering remains of dead otters and decaying fish. No one, not even the bravest warrior went there. The place reeked of evil.

Evil suited Grendel. Half-man, half-fiend, he was an extraordinary creature with supernatural strength. Covered in a green, horny skin that no sword could cut through, he came from a race of sea monsters, giants, goblins, and other outcasts from the human race.

Grendel was in the habit of sleeping for centuries, and he had been asleep so long that the king and his subjects had forgotten his existence. If they thought of him at all, they remembered him as a creature from legends. That was their big mistake.

And now the sound of music and human laughter had awakened him.

(From *Beowulf and the Monster* by Brian Patten)

Read the passage through and answer the following questions.

1 What two things was the king famous for?

2 Why was the building known as the Great Hall?

3 What do we know about Grendel? Write your answer in list form.

4 What awoke Grendel?

5 What do you think Grendel's reaction to the sound of feasting will be? Explain why you think this.

6 List five words or expressions that are typical of this type of writing.

7 Rewrite the following simple sentences, reordering the words to create different emphases. Compare your writing with the original. Which do you prefer? (You may need to make some slight changes or additions.)

It was heard by the monster, Grendel.
Grendel lived in the fens and the foul-smelling marshland beyond the forest.
The marsh was littered with oozing pools and the festering remains of dead otters and decaying fish.
Half-man, half-fiend, he was an extraordinary creature with supernatural strength.
And now the sound of music and human laughter had awakened him.

R

10 Write the next part of the tale in which Grendel awakes and makes his way to attack the Great Hall. Think about adapting sentences to create different effects. Describe his journey and the reactions of the different creatures that he passes by in the night. Describe his thoughts and feelings. You could end with these words:

Outside the Great Hall Grendel waited, silently. Crouched amongst the shadows he waited, till the last light flickered off and all was still. Then he moved towards the Hall.

Adapting a story poem

Colonel Fazackerly

Colonel Fazackerly Butterworth-Toast
Bought an old castle complete with a ghost,
But someone or other forgot to declare
To Colonel Fazack that the spectre was there.

On the very first evening, while waiting to dine,
The Colonel was taking a fine sherry wine,
When the ghost, with a furious flash and a flare,
Shot out of the chimney and shivered, 'Beware!'

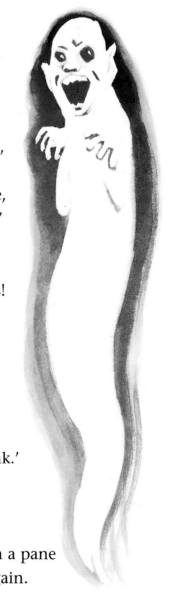

Colonel Fazackerly put down his glass
And said, 'My dear fellow, that's really first class!
I just can't conceive how you do it at all.
I imagine you're going to a Fancy Dress Ball?'

At this, the dread ghost gave a withering cry.
Said the Colonel (his monocle firm in his eye),
'Now just how you do it I wish I could think.
Do sit down and tell me, and please have a drink.'

The ghost in his phosphorous cloak gave a roar
And floated about between ceiling and floor.
He walked through a wall and returned through a pane
And backed up the chimney and came down again.

(From 'Colonel Fazackerly', *Going to the Fair*, by Charles Causley)

These are the first five verses from a poem by Charles Causley. Read them through and answer the following questions.

1 How do you know that the Colonel was not aware there was a ghost?

2 How does the author try to emphasize the ghost's movements in the second verse? Look closely at the words he uses.

3 What is the ghost trying to do to the Colonel?

4 How does the Colonel react in the third verse?

5 Why do you think that the poet mentions the 'monocle'?

6 What might 'phosphorous' mean?

7 Why do you think the ghost is roaring and racing about in the fifth verse?

8 How is each verse structured?

9 Sound out the beat to each line so that you can hear the rhythm.

10 List three ways in which this poem would have to be changed if you were to rewrite the text as a story.

11 Make a note of any key points that would need to be included in a story.

ℝ

12 Rewrite the verses, starting at verse two, changing it into a narrative. You could begin:
It was the Colonel's first evening in the castle and he was very excited. He poured himself a drink and settled down to read the newspaper before his evening meal. He had only got as far as the first page when…'

Handling nouns & pronouns

The Raven and the Whale

ONE TIME Chulyen the raven was eating fish. The more fish he ate, the hungrier he seemed to become. 'If only there was something that would satisfy this groaning ache of hunger in my belly.'

Just then he looked out to sea. A herd of whales was passing, a great school of whales, lifting and rolling in the water, lashing their tails. 'If I was to eat a whale, who knows, maybe I'd get enough meat to satisfy me and smoothen out these troublesome wrinkles of hunger.'

Chulyen opened his blue-black wings and flew over the waves. He circled in the air above the whales, flapping his wings and pondering.

Suddenly one of the whales flung itself up out of the water. It opened its mouth, it swallowed Chulyen, it crashed down into the sea.

Chulyen was falling into pitch darkness.

He was falling and falling.

Then he landed on something soft.

He rubbed his eyes. Slowly he became accustomed to the half-light. He looked about himself. He was in a red glistening cavern. High above himself he could see arched ribs stretching up into shadow. Somewhere behind the red walls a heart was beating like a great, slow, steady drum.

The only light in the cavern was coming from a softly glowing lamp.

He hopped across and looked closer; it was no more than a pool of oil with a burning wick floating in it. As the wick burned, more oil dripped down from the ceiling. It smelled sweet.

Chulyen was just leaning forwards to dip a claw into the oil and taste it, when a girl stepped out of the shadows. She was the most beautiful girl he had ever seen.

She looked at him and smiled: 'How did you come here?'

Chulyen told her how he'd been swallowed by the whale.

'What about you,' he asked, 'how did you get here?'

'Me! I've been here as long as the whale has lived. I am the spirit of the whale.'

'Tell me,' said Chulyen, 'how can I get out of this place?'

The girl laughed, a laugh as clear as tumbling water.

'How should I know that? I have never been away. I can only leave this place once, and after that there is no coming back.'

Then she looked at Chulyen with her soft brown eyes.

'But why don't you stay here? I'm lonely sometimes, living on my own. There is plenty of fish; I'll bring you as much as you can eat. But please there is one thing you must always remember: leave the lamp alone. Do not touch it.'

(From *The Song of Birds,* collected and retold by Hugh Lupton)

These are opening lines from a traditional tale from Northern America, about the Raven, a trickster.

1   What are the typical features of this traditional tale? Think about the characters and the events, and of other stories that share these features.

2   Note three examples of unusual and powerful language.

3   Chulyen thinks that he can eat the whale. What does this suggest about Chulyen?

4   Why do you think that Chulyen is warned not to touch the lamp? To answer this, think about other stories that work in the same way.

5   What is the proper noun that is repeated throughout the story?

6   From the story, make lists of:
   - five common nouns
   - five nouns in the singular
   - five nouns in the plural
   - two collective nouns
   - five pronouns

7   Continue the story in the same style. First reread the text to make it easier to imitate the style. Then when writing take care to use pronouns and nouns so that it is clear who is being talked about. Say the story to yourself occasionally, rehearsing the sentences before you write more.

The following clues may help you to structure what happens next.
   - The hungry raven does not touch the lamp but eats the oil.
   - The girl feeds him on fish.
   - The raven pecks away at the sides of the whale to get more oil.
   - He does not notice the heart beat slowing.
   - The whale dies and the raven is trapped in darkness.
   - The tale ends like this – *All that was left of it were the clean white bones rattling in the surf at the edge of the sea – and Chulyen was gone.*

Complex sentences

Old Doctor Toad

Dozing one day, Old Toad decided that he could make some money as a doctor. Why, he knew how to cure all sorts of diseases. Carefully packing a bag with medicines, Old Toad smiled to himself. This was a fine idea.

Whenever he reached a village, Old Toad would stand in the market place and call out, 'If you are ill, let me cure you.'

All the animals, including anyone who was ill, gathered round Old Toad. They wanted to be cured.

It was raining when Red Fox heard the news. Now Red Fox, who was as clever as a barrel of monkeys, looked out of his den into the night at the rain. Without worrying about getting wet, he decided to go and see Old Toad for himself. Red Fox had cut his paw on some glass and it was swollen. Slowly, he limped through the rain and darkness until he reached the market square. He could see Old Toad, who was surrounded by the animals, queuing up to be cured. However, Red Fox took one look at Old Toad, wrinkled his nose and said, 'You are nothing but warts and pimples from the top of your head to the tip of your tail – how can you claim to cure others?'

So too are many folk who forget their own defects and give advice to others.

Armenian Fable, retold by Pie Corbett

Read through this fable and then answer the questions that follow.

1 What sorts of characters were Old Toad and Red Fox?

2 Why did Red Fox go to see Old Toad and why didn't he trust him?

3 What is a moral? Explain the moral of the story of Old Doctor Toad.

4 Make a list of common features that you know are found in fables.

Remember that a main clause can stand on its own. Subordinate clauses are dependent on the main clause.

5 Write out this sentence and underline the subordinate clause that has been dropped into the main clause.
Now Red Fox, who was as clever as a barrel of monkeys, looked out of his den into the night at the rain.

6 Underline the subordinate clauses in the following sentences.
Carefully packing his bag with medicines, Old Toad smiled to himself.
Without worrying about getting wet, he decided to go and see Old Toad for himself.

7 Underline each clause in the following sentence. Circle the main clause.
He could see Old Toad, who was surrounded by the animals, queuing up to be cured.

R

8 Write your own fable, using the common features listed in your answer to question 4. You may find it useful to begin by selecting a moral from the following list:
Fools tread where the wise would never enter.
Do not play with fire or you will singe your fur.
Do not put all your eggs in one basket in case you trip.
Be kind or you will be kept company by loneliness.
Big fish swallow little fish.
Remember to use a range of complex sentences to vary your writing.

Varying sentences for interest

THE ḣEARTLESS ꙋIANT

One morning, scouting the far and deep of the castle, he came across a tiny, barred window set in the bottom of a huge grey wall. Looking through it, Leo saw nothing but dank dark pitch black. But as he turned away he imagined he heard something stir and then came a growl, a low buzz of a growl. It was a frightening sound.

His brothers told him a Giant with no heart lived in this prison with the tiny window. He didn't believe them. They were older, his brothers, and forever teasing him. But next day he went back, carrying his drum. *Rat-tat-rat-ta-ta-tat!* he played outside the window. From inside the dank dark pitch black he heard a rattle, like the rattle of a chain. He crept to the window and squinted into the shadows. Two yellow eyes the size of saucers blinked back at him. Leo jumped. A wasp buzzed angrily through the bars. Leo ran off. It was true, there was a Giant!

All night Leo thought about the Giant, his yellow eyes, the rumbling growl. Next morning he was back, *rat-tat-rat-ta-ta-tat!* on his little drum. The Giant was waiting for him….

(From *The Heartless Giant* by Jim Henson)

This is taken from the beginning of a wonder tale. Read the passage and then answer the following questions.

1   Why do you think Leo was scouting the far and deep of the castle?

2   Why do you think that the author does not use commas when he writes 'dank dark pitch black'?

3   What does the fact that the brothers tease him tell us about how Leo might feel?

4   Why do you think he played his drum outside the window?

5   Why do you think Leo returned to the Giant?

6   Write down four short, simple sentences that are used for impact, to emphasize a point.

7   Write down one sentence that uses a non-finite verb to start ('ing' or 'ed').

8   Write down one sentence that starts with *but*. Explain why you think the writer chose to write the sentence like this.

9   Write down the main clause in the first sentence. What are the extra pieces of information in the subordinate clauses?

10   Write the rest of the story. Think about what Leo will do to help the Giant. Think about the danger of having the Giant set loose. Remember to vary your sentences for interest and impact. The story ends with the words … *despite all that took place, a little boy once met a giant and they became friends.*

Varying sentence types

Fish in the Forest

Once upon a time there lived a farmer and his wife. Now, the farmer's wife could not keep a secret! Can you keep a secret? The farmer's wife, she could not keep a secret.

Anything she was told, you could be sure the whole village would know about it before the day was over. And by the end of a week – what with her travelling to market, and visiting here and there, and delivering eggs to all and sundry – by the end of a week, you could be sure that everyone in the country would know about it. And if it was a thing worth knowing, you could be certain-sure it would have reached the ears of the king.

Nothing travels faster than gossip.

Well, one day the farmer was digging turnips in a field when suddenly the blade of his spade scraped against the iron lid of a rusty old chest.

And when he lifted the lid, his eyes were dazzled by a huge hoard of sparkling, yellow gold.

'Now, now,' he thought to himself, 'I must be careful. My wife can't keep a secret. If she sees this gold, the village will know about it in a day and by the end of a week the story will have reached the ears of the king. And him being a king, and a greedy one at that, he'll want all this gold for himself.'

And the farmer sat in the field, and he thought and he thought. In the end he decided that the only thing to do was to wait for his wife to go to sleep, and then to bring the gold into the house in the middle of the night and bury it beneath the kitchen floor.

And that was what he did. He waited until she was fast asleep and snoring in her bed, and then, by the light of the moon, he crept out into the field and fetched the gold.

Carefully he carried it into the house and set to work, digging a hole in the kitchen floor.

But as he was digging, CRACK! The spade hit a rock.

His wife woke up…

(From *'Fish in the Forest'* in *Tales of Wisdom and Wonder*, retold by Hugh Lupton)

This is the beginning of a Russian traditional tale about a woman who could not keep secrets.

1 Make a list of all the elements in this story that suggest that it is a traditional tale. Think about the setting, the characters, typical objects (or creatures), what happens, and the language used.

2 How does the writer suggest that the story contains a moral and lead the reader to suppose that in the end he or she will have learned something about the importance of keeping secrets?

3 What do we know about the king's character? Why do you think kings are often shown in this light in traditional tales?

4 Find a sentence that sounds more like someone speaking than written language. Write it out and underline the part that makes it sound like speech.

5 Write out any sentence that uses an exclamation mark. Explain why you think the writer has written like this.

6 How is the writer using a question in the third sentence?

7 How many sentences begin with *And*? What is the effect of the writer starting the sentences in this way?

8 Continue the tale, writing in the same style. Vary your sentences for effect, using different sentence openings and punctuation to convey meaning.

Linking ideas in sentences

About the Moon & Moonshine

Moon

The Moon is the Earth's closest neighbour in space. But it is not a planet. Instead it is a natural satellite of the Earth.

The Moon is only about a quarter the size of the Earth. It is made of rock, and its surface is covered with huge round depressions, called **craters**. Many of these are over 100 kilometres across. The craters were made when giant lumps of rock, called **meteorites**, crashed into the Moon.

Because it is so small, the Moon has only a weak pull of gravity. This means that the Moon cannot hold any air, or atmosphere. But in 1998 the space probe *Lunar Prospector* found water ice on the Moon.

Moonshine

The Moon does not give out its own light. It only shines because it reflects light from the Sun.

The Moon circles round the Earth, while the Earth travels round the Sun. As it circles, the Moon also spins round slowly. It takes about a month for the Moon to travel around the Earth. During this time it looks as if the Moon changes from a thin crescent to a flat disc, and back again. These different shapes are called the **phases of the Moon**.

▶ Craters cover the surface of the Moon. Early astronomers thought the dark areas were oceans.

find out more

Earth
Satellites
Solar System
Space exploration
Sun

▶ The phases of the Moon. It takes around 14 days to go from a Full Moon (top) to a New Moon (bottom), and another 14 days to get back to a Full Moon again.

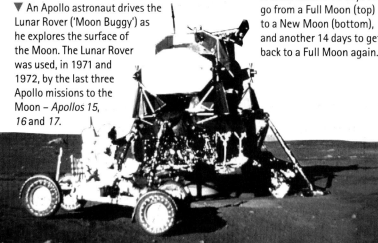

▼ An Apollo astronaut drives the Lunar Rover ('Moon Buggy') as he explores the surface of the Moon. The Lunar Rover was used, in 1971 and 1972, by the last three Apollo missions to the Moon – *Apollos 15, 16* and *17*.

(From *The Oxford Children's Pocket Encyclopedia*)

This is a report taken from an encyclopedia.

1 Why is the opening paragraph in bold and what do you think its purpose is? Why are the words **craters**, **meteorites** and **phases of the Moon** in bold?

2 What key facts does the second paragraph tell the reader?

3 The third paragraph provides an explanation. Which is the key word that helps the writer explain?

4 The writer uses the sub-heading, 'Moonshine'. What would make a useful sub-heading for the final paragraph about the Moon?

5 Is the second sentence about the Moon a proper sentence? Why?

6 Reorder this sentence. Compare the effect with the original.
*The craters were made when giant lumps of rock, called **meteorites**, crashed into the Moon.*

7 Combine these two sentences together, keeping the writing effective.
*It is made of rock, and its surface is covered with huge round depressions, called **craters**. Many of these are over 100 kilometres across.*

8 Combine these two sentences together, keeping the writing clear.
Craters cover the surface of the Moon. Early astronomers thought the dark areas were oceans.

R

9 Use these notes to write a report about the Sun. Keep the writing clear, concise and impersonal. Use features of reports, e.g. sub-headings.

- nearest star • giant gas ball • 1,392,000 km diameter • energy created in core of Sun • 16,000,000°C in core – this makes Sun shine • 1,000,000 times larger than Earth • essential to life • provides heat/light • when Moon between Sun/Earth, eclipse darkens Earth • surface temperature 6000°C

Bringing legends alive

The Children of Hamelin

IN THE YEAR 1284, a peculiar man appeared in Hamelin. He wore a bright multicolored coat, and this is why he was allegedly called Brightman. He said he was a ratcatcher and promised to free the town of all the mice and rats for a certain amount of money. The townspeople reached an agreement with him and guaranteed to pay him a particular sum for his work. Thereupon, the ratcatcher pulled out a little pipe and began blowing. All at once, the rats and mice came crawling out of the houses and gathered around him. When he thought there were none left in the homes, he started walking out of the town followed by the entire pack. After reaching the Weser River, he took off his clothes and went into the water. All the animals followed, and when they plunged into the river, they drowned.

Once the townspeople were freed from their plague, however, they regretted that they had promised to pay the man, and refused to give him any money. Instead, they made up all sorts of excuses so that he went away angry and bitter. On the 26th June, the feast of St. John and St. Paul, at seven o'clock in the morning, or at noon according to other people, he reappeared, now in the form of a hunter with a terrifying face and a strange red hat, and he began playing his pipe in all the streets of the town. This time no rats or mice appeared. Instead, the children, boys and girls from four and up, came running in large numbers, including the grown-up daughter of the mayor. The entire flock followed him, and he led them out of the town to a mountain, where they all disappeared together.

(From *Creative Storytelling* by Jack Zipes)

This is a version of a famous legend. This account provides the main events, though other different versions add more incidents.

1 Find five clues in the text that suggest this is a legend.

2 What was the mistake that the townspeople made?

3 Why do you think that they did not keep their side of the bargain?

4 Why do you think no-one stopped the children from leaving?

5 In pairs create the bare bones of the tale in note form, using a flow chart. Keep the notes clear. You do not have to use sentences – just enough words to remind you of the main points.

6 Now write some notes on why you think this tale was written. Did people in the town invent the story to cover up what really happened?

This extra information may help to give you some ideas.

- These words are inscribed on the town hall: *In the year AD 1284 130 children born in Hamelin were led out of our town by a piper and lost in the mountain.*
- There was a children's crusade in 1212.
- There was a plague brought by rats in 1284.
- Professional recruiters visited Hamelin between 1250 and 1285 and convinced many young people to resettle in the East.

R

7 Prepare a retelling of the legend based on the notes that you have made. Add in extra scenes and embellish the tale. For instance, what was the argument with the people like when they refused to pay, and did every child get lost or was one child left behind for some reason?

UNIT 18 *Investigating clauses*

The school trip

SMITHFORT SCHOOL

BUXBY
EVERPOOL

HEAD TEACHER:
MRS W ROOK

Dear Parent/Guardian

I am writing to inform you about next month's trip to Sebforn Castle. The children have been studying the Normans in Britain in History lessons this term, and this visit to the castle will help them to understand what life would have been like at that time.

The coach will leave school at 8.30am on Monday, 13th June and arrive back at 6.00pm on the same day. Children should bring a packed lunch and a drink, as this will save time at lunchtime. They may bring no more than £5.00 for snacks, gifts etc. They should wear loose, comfortable clothes and shoes for walking. Don't forget that they will be climbing on steep staircases, and walking on uneven surfaces!

The coach trip will take almost two hours. Any children who suffer from travel sickness should take medication before leaving, and bring with them medication for the home journey.

We are all looking forward to this trip. With your help, it will be one of the highlights of the school year.

Please complete and return the form below.

Yours faithfully,

W Rook

Head Teacher

- -

Trip to Sebforn Castle
(complete as appropriate)

I hereby give/do not give my permission for _____
in Class _____ to attend the trip.

(signed) _____ *(parent/guardian)*

Read through this letter and answer the following questions.

1 What reason has the Head Teacher given for the school trip?

2 Why do you think she has chosen to put this reason in the letter?

3 Suggest two reasons why the pupils may be looking forward to the trip.

4 Why does the Head Teacher mention the sort of surfaces children will be walking on?

5 Has the Head Teacher missed anything out?

6 Write a list of things you think children should take on this trip.

7 Here are three sentences from the text. Write out each one and underline its main clause.

Children should bring a packed lunch and a drink, as this will save time at lunchtime.

Any children who suffer from travel sickness should take medication before leaving, and bring with them medication for the home journey.

With your help, it will be one of the highlights of the school year.

8 Make up three complex sentences of your own about a school trip. Underline the main clause in each one.

When you have finished, swap your work with a partner and see if they agree.

R

9 Informative letters are very important for everyone. The writer must work out and include all the information that the reader will need to know.

Write a letter to a friend about a holiday outing you have arranged. Try to include as much information as possible.

Remember to check that the clauses in your sentences are well punctuated. This will give extra help to the readers.

Links within sentences

TREATING CATARACTS IN INDIA

When I was a child I often woke up panic stricken in the middle of the night. Terrified that I was blind, I would search desperately for the light switch and reassurance. I still sometimes find myself groping anxiously for the bedside light when I'm staying in a strange hotel. Fear of blindness is my worst nightmare, as it is, I know, for many others. Yet although sight is so precious, there are more than 35 million blind people in the world who could see. The problem is not just providing the treatment, but letting the blind know that it is available, and persuading them that it is safe. That is just what is being done now in India.

(Extract from an article by Mark Tully in *Second Sight Campaign* Magazine)

This is an example of some persuasive text in the form of a leaflet based around a charity for the blind. Read through the text and discuss the following questions.

1 Why do you think the writer finds the light reassuring?

2 Explain how the writer describes his fears of blindness.

3 Why might people who are blind not have this operation?

4 How do you think people reading this leaflet could help this campaign?

5 What advice would you give to someone with cataracts?

6 The writer has used lots of ways to join clauses to make complex sentences. Look at these sentences from the text, and break them down into shorter sentences.
Terrified that I was blind, I would search desperately for the light switch and reassurance.
Fear of blindness is my worst nightmare, as it is, I know, for many others.
The problem is not just providing the treatment, but letting the blind know that it is available, and persuading them that it is safe.

7 Now try putting your sentences back together in different ways to the original. For example:
I would search desperately for the light switch and reassurance because I was terrified that I was blind.

8 Write a campaign leaflet in support of a local issue. Remember that you need to persuade people to join in and help you. How can you do this?

Think carefully about how you put sentences together, and vary your sentences for interest. You could use some of the sentences from this leaflet for ideas.

Trimming sentences

Mowgli's Brothers

"Something is coming uphill," said Mother Wolf, twitching one ear. "Get ready."

The bushes rustled a little in the thicket, and Father Wolf dropped with his haunches under him, ready for his leap. Then, if you had been watching, you would have seen the most wonderful thing in the world — the wolf checked in mid-spring. He made his bound before he saw what it was he was jumping at, and then he tried to stop himself. The result was that he shot up straight into the air for four or five feet, landing almost where he left ground.

"Man!" he snapped. "A man's cub. Look!"

Directly in front of him, holding on by a low branch, stood a naked brown baby who could just walk, as soft and as dimpled a little thing as ever came to a wolf's cave at night. He looked up into Father Wolf's face and laughed.

"Is that a man's cub?" said Mother Wolf. "I have never seen one. Bring it here."

A wolf accustomed to moving his own cubs can, if necessary, mouth an egg without breaking it, and though Father Wolf's jaws closed right on the child's back not a tooth even scratched the skin, as he laid it down among the cubs.

"How little! How naked, and — how bold!" said Mother Wolf, softly. The baby was pushing his way between the cubs to get close to the warm hide. "Ahai! He is taking his meal with the others. And so this is a man's cub. Now was there ever a wolf that could boast of a man's cub among her children?"

"I have heard now and again of such a thing, but never in our pack or in my time," said Father Wolf. "He is altogether without hair, and I could kill him with a touch of my foot. But see, he looks up and is not afraid."

The moonlight was blocked out of the mouth of the cave, for Shere Khan's great square head and shoulders were thrust into the entrance. Tabaqui, behind him, was squeaking: "My Lord, my Lord, it went in here!"

"Shere Khan does us great honour," said Father Wolf, but his eyes were very angry. "What does Shere Khan need?"

"My quarry. A man's cub went this way," said Shere Khan. "Its parents have run off. Give it to me."

(From *The Jungle Book* by Rudyard Kipling)

Read the story extract through and discuss the following questions.

1 What do you think Mother Wolf heard coming up the hill?

2 Explain why Father Wolf started to leap, then tried to stop.

3 How does Mother Wolf feel about finding the man cub? How do you know?

4 What do you think the wolf family will do with the child?

5 Copy out the following three sentences into your book. Then rewrite them, trimming them so that they contain only essential information.

- *Directly in front of him, holding on by a low branch, stood a naked brown baby who could just walk, as soft and as dimpled a little thing as ever came to a wolf's cave at night.*

- *A wolf accustomed to moving his own cubs can, if necessary, mouth an egg without breaking it, and though Father Wolf's jaws closed right on the child's back not a tooth even scratched the skin, as he laid it down among the cubs.*

- *The moonlight was blocked out of the mouth of the cave, for Shere Khan's great square head and shoulders were thrust into the entrance.*

|R|

6 Rewrite this story, or another favourite story, in as few words as possible. Make sure that you include all the important information, but trim out the detail which is not necessary. When you have done this, select one or two paragraphs to rewrite as a story for younger children.

21 *Links between sentences*

A Vegetarian Diet Improves Health

Research has shown that a well-balanced, low-fat, high-fibre diet is healthier for you and your family.

As a vegetarian you could:

- Reduce your risk from certain cancers by up to 40%.

- Decrease the possibility of heart disease by over 30%.

- Restrict your chance of suffering from kidney and gall stones, diet-related diabetes and high blood pressure.

- Lower your cholesterol levels and reduce health problems related to obesity.

- Avoid fatal diseases such as nvCJD, Ecoli and food poisoning.

So why not eat your way to better health?

Food

for Life

Vegetarianism is a healthy option but it is very important to have a well-balanced diet. You could stuff your face with chips and chocolate at every meal and be vegetarian but you wouldn't be doing your health much good. It doesn't have to be rabbit food either. A varied vegetarian diet will supply all the essential nutrients you need to be fit and healthy.

This nutrition pyramid shows what types of food we should eat and roughly in what quantity and proportion.

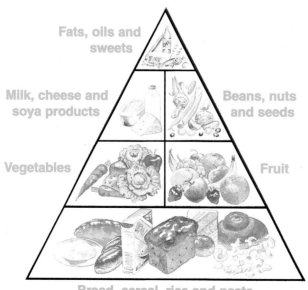

This is a copy of an internet page from the Vegetarian Society. Read through the text and discuss the following questions.

1 What do you think are the two best arguments put forward, and why?

2 Is a vegetarian diet always healthy? Give examples.

3 What do you think the writers mean by *rabbit food*?

4 Why do you think they use this phrase?

5 Which foods should we eat most often?

6 Which foods are least healthy?

7 Bullet points are one way of linking sentences. Write your own bullet-pointed list to complete the sentence:
As a cyclist you could:
Each sentence should make a separate point about why cycling is a healthy or environmentally friendly way to travel.

8 Select two sentences, e.g. from your reading book or a magazine or newspaper, and explain how they are linked.

9 We read lots of information written in a way that is meant to persuade us. Now it's your turn! Select a health issue you think is important and design a poster/web page to inform people about it, and persuade them to change their behaviour.

Remember to write in links between sentences, so that readers can follow your argument better.

Billy McBone

Billy McBone
Had a mind of his own
Which he mostly kept under his hat.
The teachers all thought
That he couldn't be taught,
But Bill didn't seem to mind that.

Billy McBone
Had a mind of his own,
Which the teachers had searched for for years.
Trying test after test,
They still never guessed
It was hidden between his ears.

Billy McBone
Had a mind of his own,
Which only his friends ever saw.
When the teacher said, 'Bill,
Whereabouts is Brazil?'
He just shuffled and stared at the floor.

Billy McBone
Had a mind of his own
Which he kept under lock and key.
While teachers in vain
Tried to burgle his brain,
Bill's thoughts were off wandering free.

Allan Ahlberg

Read the poem through and discuss the following questions.

1 What do you think the teachers thought of Billy?

2 Do you think his friends felt the same as the teachers?

3 What did the poet mean by wandering free?

4 Who do you think is writing this poem? Explain your answer.

5 Explain why Billy had a mind of his own.

6 In your workbook, make and complete a chart like this one, to show the sentences from the poem containing a subject, a verb and a prepositional phrase.

Subject	Verb	Prepositional phrase
It	was hidden	between his ears.
he	(just) shuffled (and) stared	
he	kept	
Bill's thoughts		

7 Now create another chart and fill it with your own made-up sentences that include prepositional phrases.

Subject	Verb	Prepositional phrase

R

8 Write your own poem using prepositional phrases about a child. Use the pattern of rhythm and rhyme in this poem as a pattern for your own.

You could use original ideas, or use these first lines:

Angela Brown

Came to school in a crown

VOYAGE OF THE DAWN TREADER

But this pleasant time did not last. There came an evening when Lucy, gazing idly astern at the long furrow or wake they were leaving behind them, saw a great rack of clouds building itself up in the west with amazing speed. Then a gap was torn in it and a yellow sunset poured through the gap. All the waves behind them seemed to take on unusual shapes and the sea was a drab or yellowish colour like dirty canvas. The air grew cold. The ship seemed to move uneasily as if she felt danger behind her. The sail would be flat and limp one minute and wildly full the next. While she was noting these things and wondering at a sinister change which had come over the very noise of the wind, Drinian cried, 'All hands on deck.' In a moment everyone became frantically busy. The hatches were battened down, the galley fire was put out, men went aloft to reef the sail. Before they had finished the storm struck them. It seemed to Lucy that a great valley in the sea opened just before their bows, and they rushed down into it, deeper down than she would have believed possible. A great grey hill of water, far higher than the mast, rushed to meet them; it looked certain death but they were tossed to the top of it. Then the ship seemed to spin round. A cataract of water poured over the deck; the poop and forecastle were like two drunken islands with a fierce sea between them. Up aloft the sailors were lying out along the yard desperately trying to get control of the sail. A broken rope stood out sideways in the wind as straight and stiff as if it was a poker.

'Get below, Ma'am,' bawled Drinian. And Lucy, knowing that landsmen – and landswomen – are a nuisance to the crew, began to obey. It was not easy.

(From *The Voyage of the Dawn Treader* by C.S. Lewis)

Read the story through and discuss the following questions.

1 How do you know that the storm started suddenly?

2 How does Lucy react to the change?

3 Describe how you would have felt if you had been on the ship.

4 Explain why Lucy might feel herself to be in the way.

5 Why do you think it might have been difficult for her to get off the deck?

6 Draw the following two tables in your workbook and write in the first sentence. By altering the opening, rewrite this sentence in two different ways. Then decide which is the best, and write in why.

Sentence A	There came an evening when Lucy, gazing idly astern at the long furrow or wake they were leaving behind them, saw a great rack of clouds building itself up in the west with amazing speed.
Rewrite 1	
Rewrite 2	
Which is best, and why?	

Sentence B	Before they had finished the storm struck them.
Rewrite 1	
Rewrite 2	
Which is best, and why?	

7 Write a passage about a looming disaster. For example, you might write about a storm brewing on land, or an engine failure on an aeroplane, or a rhino charge.

Remember to use a range of different sentences, paying particular attention to the way that sentences open to create atmosphere.

Punctuating complex sentences

Alice's Adventures in Wonderland

BY THIS TIME she had found her way into a tidy little room with a table in the window, and on it (as she had hoped) a fan and two or three pairs of tiny white kid gloves: she took up the fan and a pair of the gloves, and was just going to leave the room, when her eye fell upon a little bottle that stood near the looking-glass. There was no label this time with the words 'DRINK ME', but nevertheless she uncorked it and put it to her lips. 'I know something interesting is sure to happen,' she said to herself, 'whenever I eat or drink anything; so I'll just see what this bottle does. I do hope it'll make me grow large again, for really I'm quite tired of being such a tiny little thing!'

It did so indeed, and much sooner than she had expected: before she had drunk half the bottle, she found her head pressing against the ceiling, and had to stoop to save her neck from being broken. She hastily put down the bottle, saying to herself, 'That's quite enough – I hope I shan't grow any more – As it is, I can't get out at the door – I do wish I hadn't drunk quite so much!'

Alas! It was too late to wish that! She went on growing, and very soon had to kneel down on the floor: in another minute there was not even room for this, and she tried the effect of lying down with one elbow against the door, and the other arm curled around her head. Still she went on growing, and as a last resource, she put one arm out of the window, and one foot up the chimney, and said to herself, 'Now I can do no more, whatever happens. What will become of me?'

(From *Alice's Adventures in Wonderland* by Lewis Carroll)

Read through this story extract and discuss the following.

1 Why do you think Alice may have wanted the gloves and the fan?

2 Suggest a reason why Alice decided to drink from the bottle. Do you think she was wise?

3 There was no label on the bottle. If there had been, what might it have said?

4 What is the biggest problem now facing Alice?

5 Can you think of any possible solutions for Alice?

6 Find the sentence with the most punctuation marks in it. Copy the sentence into your book. List the punctuation marks, and write about why you think the writer put in each one.

7 Copy out another sentence and change it by swapping punctuation marks. Now give it to a partner to read. Discuss any differences this has made.

R

8 Write a story about a child who brushes his/her teeth with some unusual toothpaste that has a strange effect. Remember to write about what happens to them, and how they feel about it. How would you feel? Use complex sentences and punctuate them carefully to help the reader.

The Troll

Flushed with their victory, they started to run back up the passage, but as they reached the corner they heard something that made their hearts stop – a high, petrified scream – and it was coming from the chamber they'd just locked up.

'Oh, no,' said Ron, pale as the Bloody Baron.

'It's the girls' toilets!' Harry gasped.

'Hermione!' they said together.

It was the last thing they wanted to do, but what choice did they have? Wheeling around they sprinted back to the door and turned the key, fumbling in their panic – Harry pulled the door open – they ran inside.

Hermione Grainger was shrinking against the wall opposite, looking as if she was about to faint. The troll was advancing on her, knocking the sinks off walls as it went.

'Confuse it!' Harry said desperately to Ron, and seizing a tap he threw it as hard as he could against the wall.

The troll stopped a few feet from Hermione. It lumbered around, blinking stupidly, to see what had made the noise. Its mean little eyes saw Harry. It hesitated, then made for him instead, lifting its club as it went.

'Oy, pea brain!' yelled Ron from the other side of the chamber, and he threw a metal pipe at it. The troll didn't even seem to notice the pipe hitting its shoulder, but it heard the yell and paused again, turning its ugly snout towards Ron instead, giving Harry time to run around it.

'Come on, run, run!' Harry yelled at Hermione, trying to pull her towards the door, but she couldn't move, she was still flat against the wall, her mouth open with terror.

The shouting and the echoes seemed to be driving the troll beserk. It roared again and started towards Ron, who was nearest and had no way to escape.

Harry then did something that was both very brave and very stupid: he took a great running jump and managed to fasten his arms around the troll's neck from behind. The troll couldn't feel Harry hanging there, but even a troll will notice if you stick a long bit of wood up its nose, and Harry's wand had still been in his hand when he jumped – it had gone straight up one of the troll's nostrils.

(From *Harry Potter and the Philosopher's Stone* by J.K. Rowling)

Read through this story extract and discuss the following questions.

1 Why did Harry and Ron not want to go back?

2 What sort of creature was the troll? Give evidence for your answer.

3 How do you think Hermione felt when Harry told her to run?

4 Do you think Harry was brave or stupid? Explain your answer.

5 You will remember that apostrophes are used (a) to show possession (e.g. *girls' toilets*), and (b) to show that a letter or letters have been left out when words have been joined together (e.g. *they'd*). Make a chart like the one below in your workbook. Then find the words with apostrophes in the text and write them in the correct column of your chart.

Apostrophe of possession	Apostrophe for missing letter

6 Make up some sentences of your own which have words that use both kinds of apostrophe.

7 Write informally about the incident from either Hermione's or Ron's point of view. You may write it as a letter or as a diary entry. Remember to use the first person, and be careful to include and use apostrophes carefully!

Glossary

adjective   An adjective is a word that describes somebody or something.
1 Adjectives are usually found in front of a noun.
For example: *green* emeralds and *glittering* diamonds
2 In some cases, adjectives can come after a verb.
For example: It was *big.*
3 Sometimes you can use two adjectives together, e.g. *tall and handsome.* This is called an **adjectival phrase.**
4 Adjectives can be used to describe degrees of intensity. To make a **comparative** adjective you usually add *er* (or use *more*).
For example: *quick/quicker   more beautiful*
5 To make a **superlative** you add *est* (or use *most*).
For example: *quickest   most beautiful*

adverb   An adverb adds further meaning to a verb. Many are formed by adding *ly* to an adjective, e.g. *slow/slowly.* They often come next to the verb in a sentence. Adverbs can tell the reader:
How: *quickly, stupidly, amazingly.*   Where: *there, here, everywhere.*
When: *yesterday, today, now.*   How often: *occasionally, often.*

agreement   Agreement is the link between the subject of a sentence and the verb.
For example: *I am/I was   You are/you were*
The storm was becoming worse   The storms were becoming worse

apostrophe   An apostrophe (') is a punctuation mark that is used in two ways.
1 To show where letters are missing, e.g. *don't, can't, I'm.*
2 To show possession, e.g. *my dog's collar.* This explains that the collar belongs to my dog. In the plural the apostrophe follows the *s*, e.g. *the boys' cards.* This explains that the cards belonged to the boys.
There is one exception. *Its* is used for possession and *it's* stands for *it is.*

bold   Letters or words can be written in bold print, which is darker than normal. It can help to highlight words for the reader.
For example: *'Promise me, you will **never** do that again.'*

brackets   brackets can be used to add an extra comment, fact or aside into a sentence, e.g. *I am thirsty (who wouldn't be?) as a camel.*

capital letter   A capital letter starts the first word of a new sentence. It is a letter written in the upper case, e.g. JOIN NOW.

caption   A caption is a short sentence or phrase used with a picture.

classic poetry   This is poetry that has survived the test of time.

clause   A clause is a group of words that shows an event or situation. It contains a subject and a verb, e.g. *I ran.* In this clause, *I* is the subject and *ran* is the verb.

colon/   A colon is a punctuation mark (:) often used either:
semi-colon   1 To introduce a list in instructions, e.g. *You will need: two tyres ...*
2 To add further information to a sentence, e.g. *I am quick at running: as fast as a cheetah.*
A semi-colon is a punctuation mark (;) that separates two main clauses, e.g. *I like cheese; it is delicious.*

comma   A comma is a punctuation mark (,) used to separate parts in a sentence. When reading you have to leave a pause when there is a comma. Commas can be used:
1 To separate items in a list, e.g. *a sunny day, a stretch of sand, a pile of good books, several rock pools and an ice-cream van.*

2 To separate pieces of information, e.g. *That's true, yes, that's true.*

3 When addressing someone by name, e.g. *I know, Wayne.*

4 After a subordinate clause which starts a sentence, e.g. *Although it is cold, I am warm.*

5 After many connecting adverbs used to start a sentence, e.g. *However, penguins can get cold...*

comparative	See **adjective**.
conjunction	A conjunction is a word used to link clauses within a sentence, e.g. *and, but, so, until, when, as*, e.g. *He had a book in his hand when he stood up.*
connective	A connective is a word or a phrase that links clauses or sentences. Connectives can be **conjunctions** (e.g. *but, when, because*) or connecting adverbs (e.g. *however, then, therefore*).
dash	A dash is a punctuation mark (–) often used in informal writing or in place of other punctuation marks, e.g. *It was fun – we all loved it.*
definition	A definition is an explanation of the meaning of a word. For example: **purse** a small bag for holding money.
dialogue	Dialogue is the term used to describe a conversation.
discussion writing	This type of text sets out both sides of an argument and draws a conclusion, supported by reasoning and evidence. Discussion texts set out to provide a balanced argument.
exclamation mark	An exclamation mark is a punctuation mark (!) used to end an exclamation, such as joy, anger, surprise, e.g. *Oh dear!*
explanation	This type of text explains a process: how or why things happen, e.g. *How a kite flies*. Explanations hinge around the word *because* as they are based on an explanation of 'cause' and 'effect'.
full stop	A full stop (.) is a punctuation mark used at the end of a sentence.
heading	A heading is a title that may be used to show the reader what a paragraph or section of text is about.
hyphen	A hyphen is a short dash used to join words together, e.g. *snake-pit*.
instruction	This text helps readers to make something or to carry out a sequential operation.
italic	Italic writing is a writing style that slopes. It can be used to help highlight words for the reader (e.g. *Charlotte's Web* by E.B. White)
noun	A noun is a word that names something or somebody. For example: *fox, chicken, brother, rock, sea, cloud, picture.* Nouns can be singular (*dog*) or plural (*dogs*). A collective noun refers to a group, e.g. a *flock* of birds. A proper noun begins with a capital letter and names something specifically, e.g. *Mrs Brown, London*.
performance poetry	This is a form of poetry that can be performed aloud, often with music or a number of readers.
person (1st, 2nd or 3rd person)	1st person is used to talk about oneself – *I/we*. 2nd person is used to talk about whoever is listening or reading – *you*. 3rd person is used to refer to someone or somebody else – *he, she, it, they*. For example: *I* feel like *I*'ve been here for days. Look what *you* get, when *you* join the club. *He* says *it* takes real courage.
persuasive writing	This type of text intends to persuade the reader to a certain standpoint. Powerful language may be used with supporting arguments and evidence.

playscript	A playscript is the written down version of a play and is used by actors.
plural	See **singular**.
preposition	A word that suggests the position of something by place (*on, in*) or direction (*over, beyond*) or time (*during, on Friday*).
pronoun	A pronoun is a word that can replace a noun. For example: *I, me, you, he, him, she, her, we, us, it, they, them, mine, yours, his, hers, ours, theirs, its, myself, herself, himself, themselves.*
poem	A poem is a text which creates or recreates experience in a compressed and intense way, using rhythm, or rhyme and language effects to create images and sound effects.
punctuation	Punctuation is the term given to those marks used to help a reader, such as full stop (.), question mark (?), comma (,), exclamation mark (!), speech mark (' and '), colon (:) and semi-colon (;).
question mark	A question mark (?) is a punctuation mark that is used to end a question sentence. For example: *What part will you play?*
recount	This type of text tells the reader about what has happened, e.g. news, a diary.
report	This type of text provides information about a subject.
sentence	All sentences begin with a capital letter and end with a full stop, question mark or exclamation mark. A sentence must 'make sense', and be complete. There are four types: 1 *Statements* – that declare something and end in a full stop (.), e.g. *The class yelled in triumph.* 2 *Questions* – that ask something and end in a question mark (?). 3 *Exclamations* – that exclaim and end in an exclamation mark (!). 4 *Imperatives* – that command or instruct, with the verb near the start of the sentence, e.g. *Turn the knob.* Simple sentences are made up of one clause, e.g. *I am hungry.* Compound sentences are made up of two or more main clauses, joined by *and, but* or *so*, e.g. *I am hungry and I am thirsty.* Complex sentences are made up of one main clause and one, or more, subordinate clauses. A subordinate clause cannot stand on its own and relies on the main clause. It adds extra information, e.g. *I am thirsty because the well is dry.*
singular/ plural	Singular refers to one thing. Plural refers to more than one thing. For example: *dog* (singular) *sky* (singular) *wolf* (singular) *ditch* (singular) *dogs* (plural) *skies* (plural) *wolves* (plural) *ditches* (plural)
speech marks	Speech marks (' and ') are punctuation marks that enclose speech, including the relevant sentence punctuation. For example: *'What is it?' she gasped.* In direct speech you write down what is said, e.g. *'Hello children,' said Tom.* In indirect speech you report on what was said, e.g. *Tom said hello to the children.*
speech verbs	Speech verbs are the verbs used before or after speech to show how the speech has been spoken. The most common is *said*. Others include – *roared, whispered, chanted, muttered.*
standard English	Standard English is the form of English used in most writing and by educated speakers. It can be spoken with any accent. There are many slight

differences between standard English and local ways of speaking, e.g. 'We were *robbed*' is standard English but in speech some people say, '*We was robbed.*'

story   A story is a text type that recounts an invented tale. It is usually used to entertain. Stories normally have a setting, characters and are structured by a plot.

sub-heading   A sub-heading comes below a heading and indicates to the reader the contents of smaller units of text.

superlative   See **adjective**.

tense   A tense is a verb form that shows whether events happen in the past, present or the future. For example:
The Pyramids <u>are</u> on the west bank of the River Nile. (present tense)
They <u>were built</u> as enormous tombs. (past tense)
They <u>will stand</u> for centuries to come. (future tense)
Most verbs change their spelling by adding *ed* to make the past tense, e.g. *walk/walked*. Some have irregular spellings, e.g. *catch/caught*.

title   A title is the overall heading given to a text.

verb   A verb shows the action in a sentence and can express a process or state.
1 Verbs are often known as 'doing', 'being' or 'happening' words. For example, in the following sentence the word *run* is the verb.
The boys run down the hill.
2 Sometimes several words make up the verb. For instance: *The boys are running*. In this case *running* is the main verb and *are* is an extra verb that adds to the meaning. It is called an **auxiliary verb**.